For my Mother ~
who doesn't like staying in bed either!
M.C.

For Tony Downham
G.W.

Published in 1996 by Magi Publications
22 Manchester Street, London W1M 5PG

Text © 1996 Michael Coleman
Illustrations © 1996 Gwyneth Williamson

The right of Michael Coleman to be identified as the author
of this work has been asserted by him in accordance with
The Copyright, Designs and Patents Act 1988.

Printed and bound in Belgium by Proost N.V., Turnhout

ISBN 1 85430 283 3

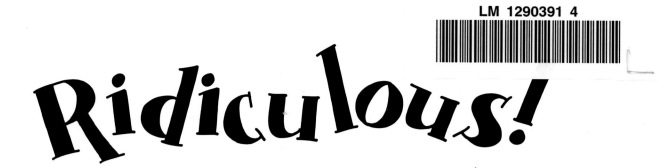

Ridiculous!

by

Michael Coleman

illustrated by

Gwyneth Williamson

"Ho-hum," yawned Mr Tortoise. "Winter is here."
"So it is," yawned Mrs Tortoise. "Come on,
Shelley, time for bed."

"But I don't feel sleepy yet," said Shelley.

"Ridiculous!" cried Mr Tortoise. "All tortoises
go to sleep for the winter."
"Why?" asked Shelley.
"Because it's cold outside and there's no food."

"But I don't want to go to sleep," said Shelley.
"I want to see what winter is like!"
"Ridiculous!" cried Mr and Mrs Tortoise together.
"Whoever heard of a tortoise out in winter?"

Soon
Mr Tortoise
began to snore . . .

. . . and not long
after that Mrs Tortoise
began to snore . . .

. . . and not long after *that*, Shelley left her warm bed of leaves, and out she went through a hole in the shed to see what winter was like.

Outside the shed, Shelley blinked.
There was snow and ice everywhere, even on the
duck pond and the hill. As she lumbered along,
a duck spotted her.

"A tortoise out in winter?" quacked the duck.
"Ridiculous!"
"No it isn't," said Shelley.
"Oh no? Then let me see you break through the
ice to get food like *I* can. Ha-quack-ha!"
"He's right," thought Shelley. "I can't do that.
I don't have a beak."

As Shelley began to walk up the hill,
she met a dog.

"A tortoise out in winter?" barked the dog.
"Ridiculous!"
"No it isn't," said Shelley, feeling a bit cross.
"Oh no? Then let me see you keep warm by
running around like *I* can. Ha-woof-ha!"
"He's right," thought Shelley sadly.
"I can't do that, either."

The dog ran off after a cat, but the cat
jumped on to the branch of a tree.
She looked down at Shelley.

"A tortoise out in winter?" mieowed the cat.
"Ridiculous!"
"No it isn't," said Shelley, even more crossly.
"Oh no? Then let me see you run into a nice warm
house as quickly as *I* can. Ha-mieow-ha!"
"She's right," thought Shelley, shivering with cold.
"I can't run like a dog or a cat. I'm much too slow!"

The cat raced off into her house before the dog could catch her, and Shelley trudged on up to the top of the hill, where she met a bird.

"A tortoise out in winter?" cheeped the bird.
"Ridiculous!"
"No it isn't," snapped Shelley.
"Oh no? Then let me see you fly off home
to cuddle up with your family like *I* can.
Ha-cheep-ha!"
"Of course I can't fly," thought Shelley.
"I can't even hop!"

Shelley felt cold and miserable. She remembered her
lovely warm bed and a tear trickled down her cheek.
"They're *all* right," she thought. "A tortoise out in
winter *is* ridiculous!"
Sadly she crept behind a shed where nobody could
see her crying . . .

. . . and slipped on a big patch of ice!
Shelley fell over backwards, and began to
slide down the hill.
Faster and faster she went . . .

. . . faster than
a *dog* could run . . .

. . . faster than
a *cat* . . .

. . . until suddenly she
hit a bump . . .

. . . and flew into the
air like a *bird*.

Wheeee!
Down she came again, and landed on the
icy duck pond. She slithered towards her hole
in the shed . . .

. . . but it was all covered up with ice!
"Ha-quack-ha, what did I say? Where's your
beak to break the ice with?"
The duck fell about laughing.
"No, I don't have a beak," thought Shelley.
"But I *do* have . . .

. . . *a shell!*"
And tucking her head inside it,
Shelley smashed her way through the ice,
into the shed and home!

Mrs Tortoise woke up as she heard all the noise.
"You haven't been outside, have you, Shelley?"
she asked.
"Outside?" said Shelley, snuggling into bed.
"Whoever heard of a tortoise out in winter?"

And before you could say
'Ridiculous!'
Shelley was fast asleep.